CRAWLEY
TO
LITTLEHAMPTON

Vic Mitchell and Keith Smith

FOREWORD

It is a pleasure to contribute a few words to another of Vic Mitchell and Keith Smith's excellent books on the railways in South East England. This volume, the first to deal exclusively with the Arun Valley Line, is published to coincide with the joint venture between the West Sussex County Council and British Rail to promote the use of this scenic route through the beautiful West Sussex countryside.

The railway fulfils an important commuter need in Network SouthEast and in addition provides ideal access to important tourist attractions including Amberley Chalk Pits Museum, Arundel Castle and Arundel Wildfowl Trust.

Enjoy the book and experience a journey through West Sussex at its best.

Peter G Shepherd
Chairman West Sussex County Council

Chichester
July 1986

Charles H Attwell
Area Manager British Rail

First published – August 1986

Design – Deborah Goodridge

ISBN 0906520 34 7

© Middleton Press, 1986.

Published by Middleton Press
    Easebourne Lane
    Midhurst, West Sussex.
    GU29 9AZ
    ☎ 073 081 3169

Typeset by CitySet · Bosham 573270

Printed & bound by Biddles Ltd,
        Guildford and Kings Lynn.

CONTENTS

ACKNOWLEDGEMENTS

We would like to thank the photographers noted in the captions for much help received, and also C. Attwell, I. Dean, J. Chamberlain, H. Hunt, Sir Norman and Peter Longley, R. Resch, R.C. Riley, David Smith, D. Waghorn, and Mrs. E. Wallis. As usual, our gratitude for assistance in production must be expressed to Mrs. E. Fisk, N. Langridge, R. Randell, N. Stanyon and our ever helpful wives.

GEOGRAPHICAL SETTING

The first summit on the line is at Faygate, where the watershed between the River Mole and the River Arun is reached. The route from Crawley to the outskirts of Pulborough traverses the undulating Wealden Clays, with the exception of an area of sandstone around Horsham, formed by the Hastings Beds which underly Ashdown Forest. At Pulborough, cuttings take the track through the sandy ridges of the Hythe and Sandgate Beds before it descends onto the broad floor of the Arun Valley. The Arun Gap in the South Downs was an obvious route for the railway surveyors, the only obstacle on the way to the coast being a projection of chalk south of Amberley, which necessitated a short tunnel. A similar problem arose north of Boxhill where the line from London passed through the North Downs.

All maps contained in this album are to the scale of 25″ to 1 mile, unless otherwise stated.

(Railway Magazine)

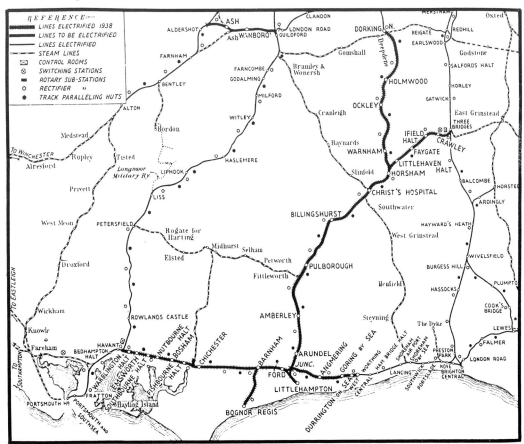

HISTORICAL BACKGROUND

The first railway to Horsham was a branch from the London to Brighton line at Three Bridges, with intermediate stations at Crawley and Fay Gate (later one word). It was opened for traffic on 14th February 1848. This line was extended to Petworth on 10th October 1859 with stations at Billingshurst and Pulborough only.

The Brighton to Portsmouth line was built in 1840-47 but it was not until 3rd August 1863 that it was linked to the Petworth branch by a line through Arundel and Amberley from Ford Junction. The branch from there to Littlehampton was opened two weeks later. In 1887, the junction was altered to allow through running to and from the north and east instead of only Ford.

All the lines mentioned were operated by the London Brighton and South Coast Railway. Its successor, the Southern Railway, electrified the routes between Dorking and Three Bridges, in the north, and Havant and West Worthing, in the south, on 30th June 1938. Regular electric services on these lines and the Littlehampton and Bognor Regis branches began on 2nd July 1938.

The route south of Horsham was misleadingly known as the *Mid-Sussex*, but on 24th March 1986 it was officially renamed the *Arun Valley Line*.

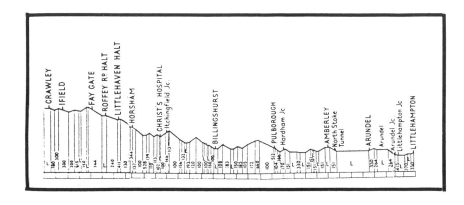

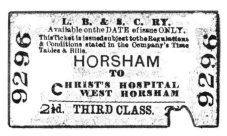

PASSENGER SERVICES

The service on the Horsham branch in 1853 consisted of 5 journeys on weekdays and 2 on Sunday. By mid-1859 this had increased to 8 and 4 respectively and with the extension of the line to Petworth later that year there were 10 trains on weekdays to Horsham, half of which continued to the new terminus.

The initial service on the Arundel line was only three a day and these were run at reduced speed owing to the trackbed being unconsolidated. Eventually, the weekday timetable settled down to 5 trains to Portsmouth; 2 to Petworth and 3 to Horsham only.

By 1869, the route south of Horsham was seeing 6 stopping trains (plus one express stopping only at Arundel) on weekdays, with 2 trains on Sundays. Twenty years later the service had increased by 50% and Littlehampton had 21 departures on weekdays (9 on Sundays) for Ford or Arundel.

In 1910, the Mid-Sussex line had 12 trains on weekdays and 4 on Sundays. Between Three Bridges and Horsham there were 4 additional push-pull trains providing the "Motor Car Service" on weekdays, calling at the halts opened on 1st June 1907 at Ifield, Littlehaven and Roffey Road.

The departures southwards from Horsham in July 1924 make an interesting study for their variety.

Weekdays

a.m.
7.43	semi-fast to Portsmouth
7.53	all stations to Midhurst
9.28	all stations to Chichester
10.13	express to Portsmouth
10.25	all stations to Bognor
11.26	semi-fast to Bognor

p.m.
12.23	express to Bognor
1.12	all stations to Bognor
1.38	all stations to Midhurst
2.18	(from London Bridge) express to Bognor, with Pullman Luncheon Cars for Littlehampton detached at Ford.
2.44	all stations to Littlehampton

3.27	express to Portsmouth
4.31	all stations to Midhurst
5.25	express to Bognor, with Pullman Tea Cars
5.30	all stations to Littlehampton
5.49	express to Bognor (from London Bridge)
6.06	express to Portsmouth
6.27	all stations to Littlehampton
7.16	express to Bognor
7.23	Billingshurst and Pulborough only
8.41	all stations to Portsmouth

Sundays

a.m.
9.01	all stations to Midhurst
9.40	express to Bognor
9.55	all stations to Bognor
10.23	semi-fast to Portsmouth

p.m.
8.14	all stations to Portsmouth
8.27	all stations to Midhurst

Electrification in 1938 brought dramatic increases and regular intervals to the timetable. An hourly express from Victoria ran via Dorking (except three journeys run via Three Bridges) calling at Horsham, Arundel and Barnham where it divided for Bognor Regis and Portsmouth Harbour. A half-hourly stopping service was provided between Three Bridges and Littlehampton – alternate trains reversing and continuing to Bognor. All Midhurst trains terminated at Pulborough and a shuttle service between Arundel and Littlehampton was provided to connect with the London expresses.

Some reductions took place in World War II, particularly with regard to buffet facilities on the express services. In 1966 some fast trains were withdrawn but in the following year they were reinstated, although the stopping service was reduced to hourly.

In 1978 most of the express services were diverted to call at Gatwick Airport but in 1984 these were withdrawn, leaving a basic hourly stopping service south of Horsham, with a few irregular additional trains and only a few trains with buffets. Christs Hospital and Amberley stops were omitted by many of the trains, although an hourly service was restored to the latter station in 1986.

CRAWLEY

1. An eastward view reveals the delicate nature of the canopy brackets; bustles and bowlers, and a lady with her back to the child who is almost impaled on the fence. (Lens of Sutton)

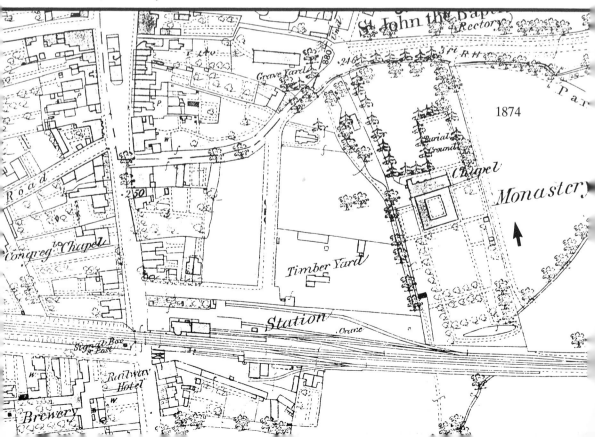

2. A postcard view in the opposite direction shows horse boxes in the up bay and the extensive stables behind the Railway Hotel. (Lens of Sutton)

1910 map showing a siding into the timber yard of James Longley & Co and their narrow gauge line from the timber stock yard crossing it. Longleys have long been involved in the building of railway stations. For example they constructed all the stations on the Cuckoo Line and the recent replacement at Polegate.

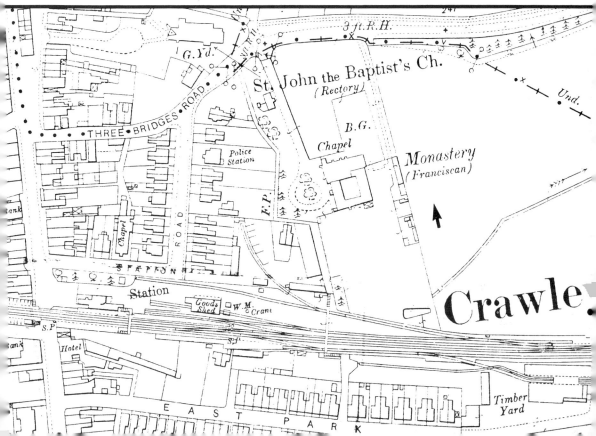

3. The footbridge in the distance spanned the goods yard but was not shown on the 1874 map. Another horse box is to be seen – agricultural traffic would have provided much of the revenue here, as the population of the town was under 500 at the turn of the century. (Lens of Sutton)

4. With the Railway Hotel on the right and The Capital and Counties Bank on the left, class E6 0–6–2T no.407 departs towards Horsham. This 61-ton locomotive was built in 1904 and named *Worplesdon*. (Lens of Sutton)

5. This signal box replaced an earlier smaller structure which stood by the station's only signal (see 1874 map). Closure took place on 20th April 1986 but since 1978 it was a crossing box controlling lifting barriers and not a block post. Plans are being made to retain the structure as part of the town's history. The barriers are now supervised under CCTV by Three Bridges signal panel.
(G. Holmes collection)

London Brighton & South Coast Railway.

Amberley to

Red Hill

6. Looking west from the footbridge in June 1923, we can see that E. Constable had parked his horse-drawn timber bolsters with half their length protruding through the fence. A nice point in law. (Late E. Wallis)

7. A 1958 photograph from the footbridge shows the 1938 extension of the goods yard. On the right is Longley's steam saw mills. Imported pitch pine was brought by rail from Surrey Docks; transferred to narrow gauge wagons for movement to the stock yard and returned that way to the works when required, mainly for the production of flooring blocks. Coal for the works was also received at the siding. (D. Cullum)

8. Parcel vans stand in the bay as standard class no.41301 passes the busy goods yard with a Horsham to Three Bridges freight on 4th June 1965. The crane on the right was rated at 4½ tons. The "New Crawley Goods Yard" is on the main line between Three Bridges and Gatwick Airport. (S.C. Nash)

9. Construction of a new station was well advanced in February 1968. The goods yard had been largely cleared, only the crane plinth remaining at this stage. Earlier, a siding had curved northwards, passing through a gate to serve the coal staithes of M. Nightingale, shown on the map. (E. Wilmshurst)

10. The old station is seen on its last day in use – 27th July 1968. The covered lattice foot-bridge above milepost 30¾ was a standard LBSCR design – a similar one stands at Chichester, although now devoid of a roof. (J. Scrace)

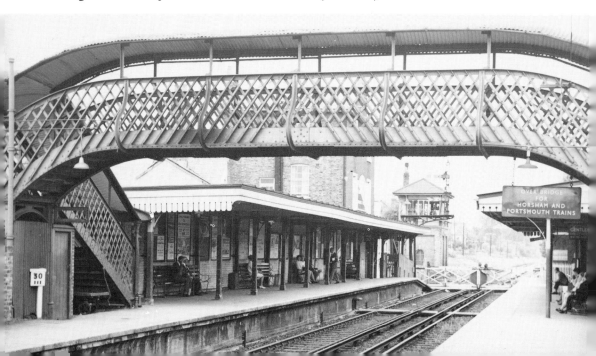

11. Another last day view shows a stopping train to Bognor Regis. At this time, the other train in each hour was a slow to Horsham only. The station house on the left is thought to date from the opening of the line and the offices behind the distant signal dated from 1967, being erected above the new station. (J. Scrace)

12. The plain but functional form of the new station is observed from the public footbridge steps, four days before trains started to call there. The car park on the left was built, in the words of the ballad, "in a monastery garden". (D. Cullum)

13. Relief Gateman W.G. Brown peers out of no. 7 Crossing Box on 26th June 1923. The gates were superseded by lifting barriers, supervised by CCTV from Crawley box, on 21st August 1977. Since April 1986, the monitors have been in Three Bridges signalling centre. (Late E. Wallis)

14. A halt was opened here on 1st June 1907. It was known as Lyons Crossing Halt but became "Ifield Halt" only five weeks later, the "halt" being dropped in 1930. The short platforms were extended with the introduction of electric services. (D. Cullum)

London Brighton and South Coast Railway,

Arundel to

Gillingham

15. Another 1969 photograph shows the crossing keeper's cabin and cottage. The gates were opened by hand when required, the plate on the post bearing the words *RING THE BELL*. Such facilities were inappropriate as Crawley New Town spread over the area and so a road bridge was built a little to the east. (D. Cullum)

16. Chipmans operate their weed-killing service over a large part of British Rail's network from their Horsham depot. This train is passing through Ifield, bound for Gloucester on 24th April 1973 and is headed by no. E6025. (J. Scrace)

17. A 1973 photograph reveals the transformation of the up platform facilities that nearly turned it into a suburban station was it not for the country halt iron shed retained on the opposite platform. The new road bridge is in the background and the severed road is either side in the foreground. (J. Scrace)

London Brighton & South Coast Railway.

Littlehampton to

REIGATE

(S. E. & C. R., via Red Hill)

18. By 1983, the down side shelter had been modernised. A 4CIG unit, destined for Bognor Regis via Littlehampton, passes under the foot bridge erected after the level crossing was abolished. (J.S. Petley)

FAYGATE

19. Another unusual train was photographed just west of the station, at the same location as the weed-killing train. This is a special from the Electrical Engineer's depot at Horsham on 16th May 1983 setting off to collect electrical equipment from the Sanderstead-Woodside line which had closed the previous week. (J.S. Petley)

20. Unlike its present neighbours, this station remains surrounded by fields. Milk and other agricultural traffic produced good revenue – passengers never have. Terrier no. 659 (prior to 1901 no. 59 *Cheam*) propels its single coach "Motor Train" towards Horsham. (Lens of Sutton)

1911 map showing the position of the goods crane (Cr.), which was of 4½ ton capacity, as at Crawley.

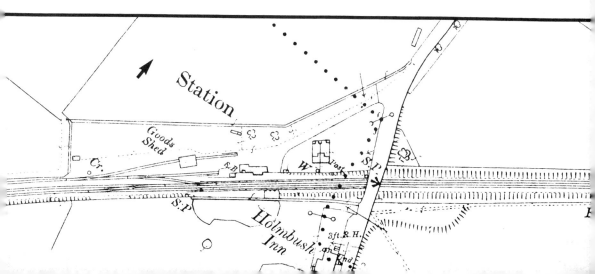

21. The station house was built in 1847 at a cost of £1050 and the passenger area was later extended. To reduce manpower, an extension was added to the signal box so that the signalman could issue tickets from it, whilst passengers stood under the lean-to shelter. (Lens of Sutton)

22. Class N no. 31401 hauls the Horsham to Three Bridges freight on 10th May 1965, passing by the deserted local goods yard which closed on 8th November 1961. (J. Scrace)

23. The SR added the concrete footbridge and the upper quadrant signal which is silhouetted against the white sighting panel on the road bridge. Although the 1911 Ordnance Survey showed Faygate as one word, the railway continued to use Fay Gate until December 1953. (J. Scrace)

London Brighton & South Coast Railway.

Arundel to

Chelsea

24. The lean-to provided for passengers booking tickets was eventually enclosed, resulting in this charming hybrid. The signal box ceased to function on 20th April 1986 and Faygate became the boundary between the Horsham and Three Bridges boxes. (J. Scrace)

London Brighton & South Coast Railway.

Littlehampton to

Forest Hill

ROFFEY ROAD HALT

25. The halt opened with the others on the branch on 1st June 1907 but closed on 3rd January 1937. It was temporarily out of use between January 1917 and May 1920. This undated photograph of class E5 no. 2953 shows the down platform in the distance. The railway cottages are also visible and were demolished in 1972. Automatic half barriers replaced the gates in 1965.
(D. Cullum collection)

26. On 18th February 1984, trains were diverted from the Brighton main line due to engineering works. In the foreground, we see the remains of the supports of the waiting shelter. Similar evidence remains of Monks Lane Halt, north of Edenbridge Town.
(P.G. Barnes)

LITTLEHAVEN

27. Opened as Rusper Road Crossing Halt on 1st June 1907, the name was changed to Littlehaven Crossing Halt after only a few weeks and finally settling on Littlehaven Halt by the end of the year. "Halt" was dropped in May 1969. Unlike Ifield and Faygate, the ticket office was erected on the down platform. (Lens of Sutton)

29. Wimblehurst Lane level crossing was replaced by automatic half barriers in March 1977, when the name was changed to Parsonage Road. This photograph was taken in 1974 – by then the area south of Littlehaven had been built up to join Horsham. (J. Scrace)

28. A 1968 view shows the basic facilities provided. By 1972, a complete rebuilding had taken place although the gates still remained in use in 1986, awaiting the re-profiling of the road prior to the provision of automatic half barriers. (J. Scrace)

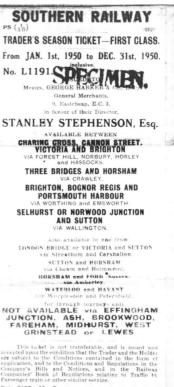

HORSHAM

THE EXTERIOR HORSHAM RAILWAY STATION.

30. This handsome facade greeted impending passengers from 1859 until 1938. It was part of the second station; its predecessor was situated a little to the north of it. (Lens of Sutton)

31. West Box was situated at the south end of the station – its position is marked S.B. on the map. It was in use from 1875 until 1938. Its signalman can see little more than the smoke and clerestory roofs of this special train. (Lens of Sutton)

32. Looking south from North Street bridge we can see West Box in the distance and Shunting Box in the foreground. The latter was not marked on the map. The cattle pens on the right were on the site of the first locomotive shed. The docks were later adapted for parcel and mail traffic but are seldom used today. (Lens of Sutton)

London Brighton & South Coast Railway.

Littlehampton to

BARCOMBE MILLS

33. The shedmaster (under the bowler hat) poses with his shed staff and footplate crews – not forgetting the wheel tapper (extreme right). The date and names have not survived the passing of time. (LBSCR)

34. The round house was partly completed in 1896 and eventually had 18 bays radiating from the central turntable. This view was taken in about 1920, long before the coal stage on the right was supplied with a crane. Other features of interest include the brazier to prevent the water column freezing; ash pits in both turntable roads; a water softening plant on top of the tank and a grounded coach body for Shed staff. (M.G. Joly collection)

35. Jack "The Wheeltapper" Harrod leans on a Lancashire & Yorkshire Railway wagon in Horsham Yard in February 1936 having found a split tyre. There were no Health & Safety Inspectors to insist on safety props in those days – speed was top priority. (F.G. Holmes)

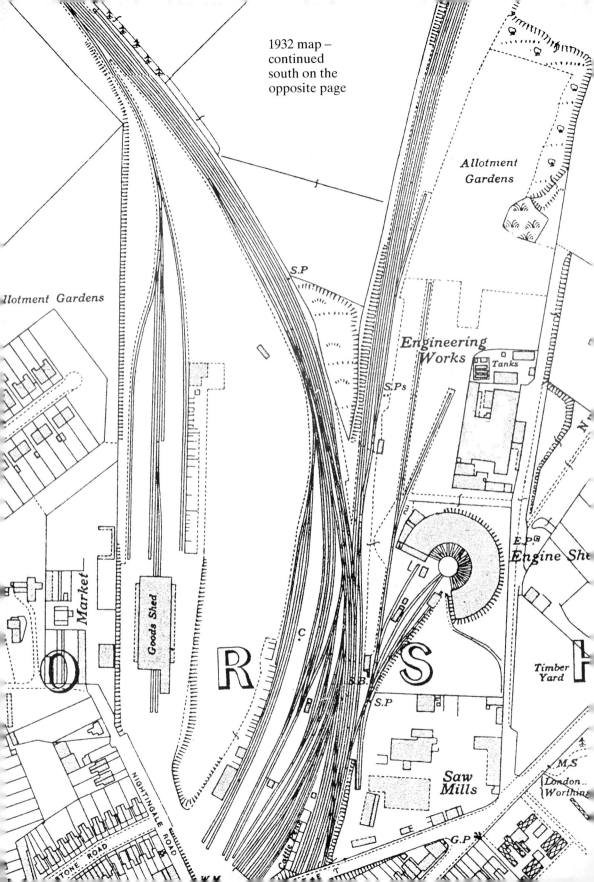

1932 map –
continued
south on the
opposite page

Allotment
Gardens

llotment Gardens

S.P

Engineering
Works

Tanks

S.Ps

E.P.

Engine She

Market

Goods Shed

O

R

S

Timber
Yard

C.

S.B.

S.P

M.S

London..
Worthin

Saw
Mills

G.P

NIGHTINGALE ROAD

STONE ROAD

Castle Pla

36. The main line from Dorking is in the left background whilst the "branch" from Three Bridges is right of centre. The station pilot is about to pass the Junction Box on the up main line whilst, on the right, an LMS wagon stands on the 80ft long siding to Agates saw mill, circa 1933. (Lens of Sutton)

37. An electrification train comes off the branch on 2nd October 1937, hauled by class C3 no. 2301. The Portsmouth No. 2 scheme comprised the electrification of 165 track miles (75 route miles) at a cost of £2.75M. (H.C. Casserley)

38. During 1938, the station was completely rebuilt and the pedestrian subway, shown on the map, was replaced by a footbridge. This is the north end of the platform under reconstruction on 17th July 1938, whilst class D no. 2625 runs in with a local train. (H.C. Casserley)

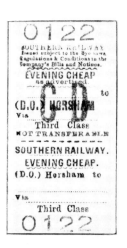

39. Looking south from the temporary foot-bridge on the same day, we witness the arrival of a train from Brighton, hauled by class I3 no. 2026. Colour light signalling, con-trolled from one box instead of three, was switched on on 24th April 1938, in readiness for the more frequent electric services. (H.C. Casserley)

40. Single line working on the down line was necessary on 30th March 1958 whilst the up junction was relaid. The 10.45 Bognor Regis to Three Bridges passes by at reduced speed whilst haze rises from the round house. (D. Cullum)

42. The controversial and unconventional exterior was described in Nairn's *Buildings of England* as "the most horrible front". This 1958 view shows the bold lettering which has been altered several times since. (D. Cullum)

Other views and maps of this station are to be found in our *Branch Lines to Horsham* and *Epsom to Horsham* albums.

41. Three electric locomotives were built and were used mainly on freight services. This is no. 20002, bound for Chichester on 4th July 1958. Some electrified sidings were provided at Norwood Junction, Horsham and Chichester for these locomotives. (J. Scrace)

43. An interesting comparison can be made between this 1959 view and photograph no. 32 which was taken from the same location. All four platforms were lengthened to over 800ft and three electric carriage sidings were provided (visible on the left), with three more south of the station. (J. Scrace)

45. No. 3021 was one of 17 six-car units which included a pantry car. They normally operated from London to Eastbourne, to Brighton and to Littlehampton via Hove. In 1965, two units were diagrammed for the 9.18am Victoria to Bognor Regis service only, returning empty to Littlehampton. 4COR sets operated the expresses services for around 30 years, examples appearing in *Epsom to Horsham* in pictures 35 and 113. (J. Scrace)

44. Class C2X operated many of the local freight services, as far afield as Midhurst. No. 32523 waits, as the shadows lengthen, to depart with the 7.24pm to Three Bridges on 24th August 1959. (J. Scrace)

46. For over 30 years Chipmans have been operating their weed-killing trains from a depot in the goods yard. Between mid-April and late July they cover about half of BR, treating around 10,000 track miles and 2000 miles of bank at speeds up to 45mph. Former SR Maunsell coach no. S6697 is seen as no. CWT11 in 1973; subsequently it moved to the Mid-Hants Railway for restoration to passenger services. (J. Scrace)

47. The goods yard ceased to handle general traffic on 4th May 1970 but much of the track was retained. Present users include Chipmans, UK Fertilisers, the Electrical Engineer and Shell (UK) Oil, whose sidings we see on the south side of the Crawley line, in May 1973. (J. Scrace)

48. The Royal Train carrying the Queen from Brighton to Portsmouth Harbour on 19th July 1985 travelled an unusual route via Three Bridges and Horsham. The locomotive was the usual one for special occasions – no. 73142 *Broadlands*. Industrial premises now occupy the site of the roundhouse. (J. Scrace)

49. The Horsham bypass was constructed in 1963. This is the scene on 19th May, less than ½-mile north of Christs Hospital, when the bridge beams were put in position. (D. Cullum)

CHRISTS HOSPITAL

50. In 1897, the governors of Christs Hospital decided to move the school out of London and the LBSCR opened a new station on 1st May 1902 to serve it and an anticipated housing development to be known as West Horsham. The latter never came about and the former became a boarding school seldom requiring the lavish station provided. (Lens of Sutton)

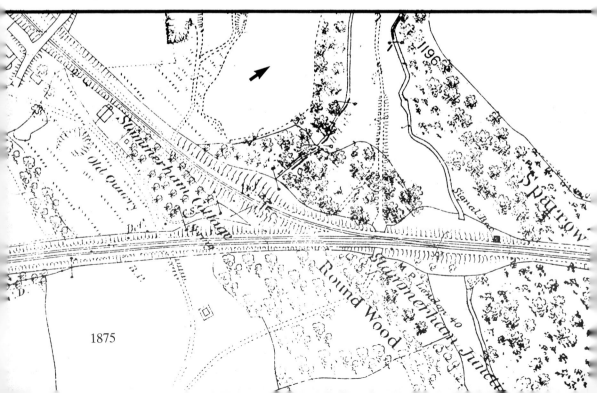

1875

51. The goods facilities were equally excessive with five sidings and this impressive goods shed with a 1½-ton crane. The yard was little used latterly and closed in September 1961. Eight cottages were built for railway staff – a few are visible on the right. (Lens of Sutton)

52. The line to Cranleigh and Guildford is seen on the left of this 1922 photograph, taken from the top of the up main starting signal. Until the opening of the station Stammerham Junction signal box stood beyond the crossover, on the left. (Late E. Wallis)

53. The extent of the "Bluecoat School" is difficult to imagine without a photograph. On the left is the original Itchingfield Junction Box which was some way north of the junction and survived until about 1920.

Longleys built both the station and the school. For the latter, five *acres* of their patented wood block flooring was brought by rail from their Crawley siding.
(D. Cullum collection)

54. The main (and infrequent) use for Platform 1 (on the right) was the reception and despatch of pupils' trunks each term or an occasional special train for the school. The main Mid-Sussex lines are on the left of this 1957 photograph. (D. Cullum)

55. South Box or "B Box" is in the distance – it controlled the exit from the down loop and access to the goods yard. It was therefore seldom staffed and was closed in 1961. "A Box" was still staffed in 1986, serving as a booking office also. The distant banner repeater signal was no longer needed. (Lens of Sutton)

1911 map shows a curved embankment in the top left corner that carried a spur line which formed a triangular junction for a few years but the dates are uncertain.

56. The 11.06 Victoria to Bognor Regis departs on 20th September 1969 almost three years before the mammoth act of vandalism took place when BR destroyed this fine station. Fortunately, those in power are now less blinkered and are finding other uses for redundant buildings. Only the waiting room on platform 2 remained and this was adapted to house toilets and a booking office. (J. Scrace)

L. B. & S. C. & L. & S. W. Rys.
Available for 2 Days including date of issue
CHRIST'S HOSPITAL W.H. TO
SOUTHAMPTON [WEST]
Via HAVANT & L. & S. W. Ry.
5s. 0½d. THIRD CLASS. 5s. 0½d.
The connection of trains not guaranteed
Not transferable ... issued subject to the
Conditions in the Time ... s of the respective
Co's over whose lines ... ticket is available.

0232   0232

London Brighton & South Coast Railway.

Christ's Hospital to

Fratton

57. This is the signalman's view from Itchingfield Junction Box on 4th June 1962, when class E4 no. 32503 and E6 no. 32417 headed an LCGB railtour. The lines to Shoreham on the right were closed on 5th March 1966 and feature in our *Branch Lines to Horsham*, along with the Guildford branch from Christ's Hospital. (J. Scrace)

58. The nameboard on the small signal box at Barns Green was mis-spelt Barnes Green until it was abolished in favour of automatic half barriers in July 1965. This 1923 photograph shows two gates across the road and two swung away from it. (Late E. Wallis)

BILLINGSHURST

59. Looking towards Horsham in 1922, we can appreciate the rural nature of the station with a profusion of milk churns on the down platform and a narrow lane leading to Great Daux Farm. This is now a busy road in Daux Industrial Estate. Messrs Narge's private siding curved away through the white gate. (Late E. Wallis)

1897

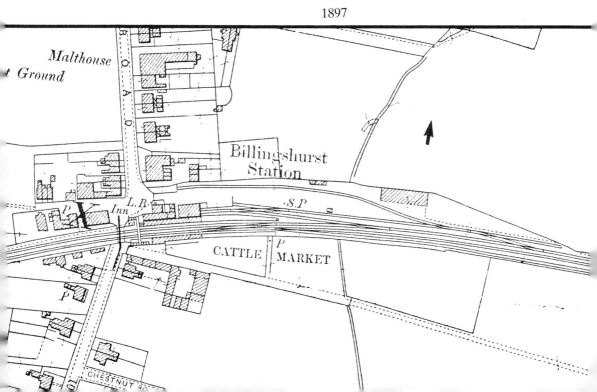

60. Upon opening, the station was "rustically situated in a ploughed field", according to a contemporary account. Eventually a lane was constructed by the LBSCR to link to the Roman road which passed through the village over ½-mile away. Another 1922 view shows the goods shed to be attached to the main building, as at Pulborough. (Late E. Wallis)

61. Although less imposing than its contemporary at Pulborough, the building deserves a place in the history of the town as the one having more effect on the development of the district than any other. Little change has occurred since this photograph was taken in 1962. (D. Cullum)

62. The down platform canopy has been further reduced and the goods yard was closed to general traffic on 4th May 1964, although a siding was retained for a while by the Express Dairy Co. (Lens of Sutton)

63. The signal box is one of the earliest LBSCR boxes to remain in use in 1986 and as such is important local and railway history. It has had controlled barriers since 1978 when the road was widened. (J. Scrace)

64. A northward view of Adversane crossing in March 1924 reveals that the Down Home signal arm had been removed. This was normal practice for the duration of the winter timetable. (Late E. Wallis)

London Brighton & South Coast Railway.

Henfield to

CHRIST'S HOSPITAL

(WEST HORSHAM)

65. At this time, the gateman was George Piper. Automatic half barriers were introduced in 1966, protected by the usual colour light signals. Twenty years later, drivers were still confronted by a mixture of signalling as Christs Hospital, Billingshurst, Pulborough and Amberley retained largely oil-lit semaphores, within station limits. (Late E. Wallis)

66. The railway was often obliged to provide and maintain unnecessary crossings. Cray Lane is an example – a bridge is within sight, in the background. A southward view taken on 30th April 1925. (Late E. Wallis)

67. Signalman Charles Pope poses on the same day. The nameplates on the Tyer's Block Instruments in Billingshurst, Adversane and Pulborough boxes were all mis-spelt Gray Lane. AHBs took over in 1966. (Late E. Wallis)

PULBOROUGH

68. Terminating trains from Midhurst used the left hand face of the island platform. In the hey-day of the LBSCR, the down platform received slip coaches for Midhurst, shed at speed from a Portsmouth-bound express. (Lens of Sutton)

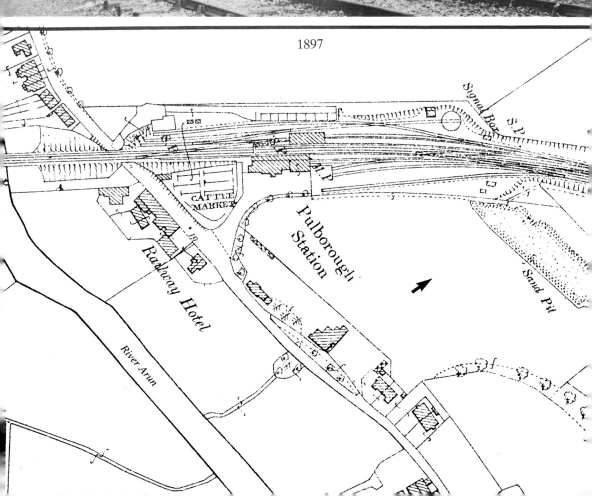

1897

69. Looking north in 1923, we can see the conveniently situated cattle market on the right and a driveway on the left which led to the railway's cattle dock and pens. Passengers and general goods used the approach on the opposite side of the line, avoiding the embarrassing conflict that often occurred at other stations. (Late E. Wallis)

70. The turntable was little used in later years of the Midhurst branch as most services were worked by push-pull trains. The photograph is undated but the cleanliness of the insulators suggest 1938. (J.W.R. Kirkby)

72. Class E4 0–6–2T no. 32564 pulls its assorted goods train out of the loop on 14th June 1961, on its way back to Horsham. Until 1951, it ran outwards to Midhurst via Arundel, Chichester and Singleton. (R.A. Holder)

71. The platforms were lengthened at the southern ends just prior to electrification and the subway entrance on the up side had to be moved and re-roofed. Compare this with the earlier view. A Midhurst push-pull stands in the loop on 14th August 1954, six months before the service was withdrawn. (D. Cullum)

73. The de-icing unit stands in the loop in the early morning sun on 4th March 1967. The loop was severed at its southern end and retained as an engineer's siding. (J. Scrace)

74. This facade has changed little since photographed in 1974. The former goods yard and cattle market have been resurfaced to make good car parks and, as at Christs Hospital, Billingshurst and Arundel, a commercial use has been found for the goods shed. (J. Scrace)

75. Electric enthusiasts will be surprised to find 4 CAP no. 3202 bound for Victoria in 1981. These units were then normally exclusively used on Coastway services. The down train is an express for Bognor Regis. (W. Walker)

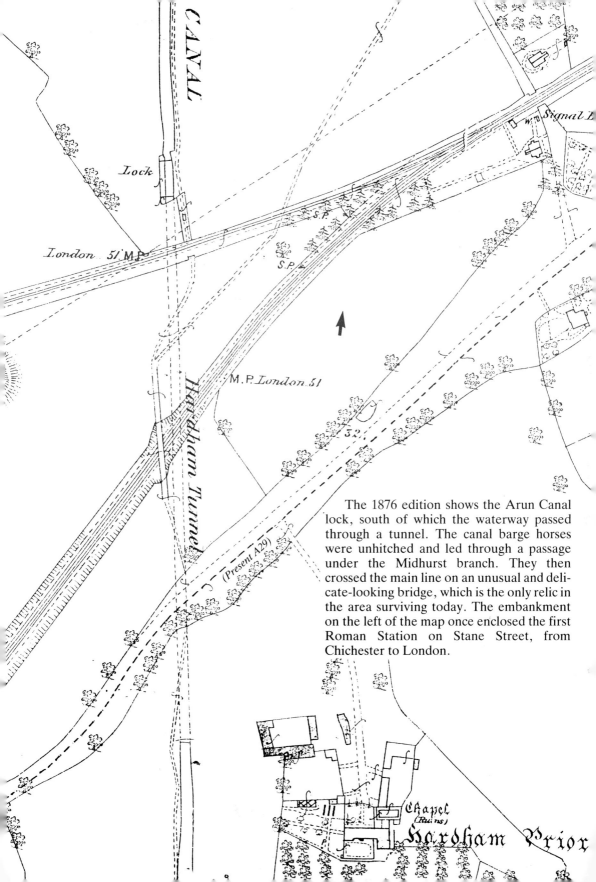

CANAL

Lock

London 51 M.P.

S.P.

S.P.

Hardham Tunnel

M.P. London 51

32.

(Present A29)

Signal L

The 1876 edition shows the Arun Canal lock, south of which the waterway passed through a tunnel. The canal barge horses were unhitched and led through a passage under the Midhurst branch. They then crossed the main line on an unusual and delicate-looking bridge, which is the only relic in the area surviving today. The embankment on the left of the map once enclosed the first Roman Station on Stane Street, from Chichester to London.

Chapel (Ruins)

Hardham Prior

76. A damaged photograph from 1921 shows Hardham Junction, which was nearly one mile from Pulborough. The Midhurst branch converges to single line and a siding passes through a gate for the benefit of the adjacent estate. (Late E. Wallis)

77. The signal box was one of the last to display the stilts – a once common LBSCR feature. Other views of Pulborough and this junction are to be found in our *Branch Lines to Midhurst*. (E.R. Lacey collection)

78. Thorndell Box was on the up side, south of Coldwaltham, and is seen here in July 1965. It was prone to flooding in winter, being adjacent to an area known as Amberley Wild Brooks. (D. Cullum)

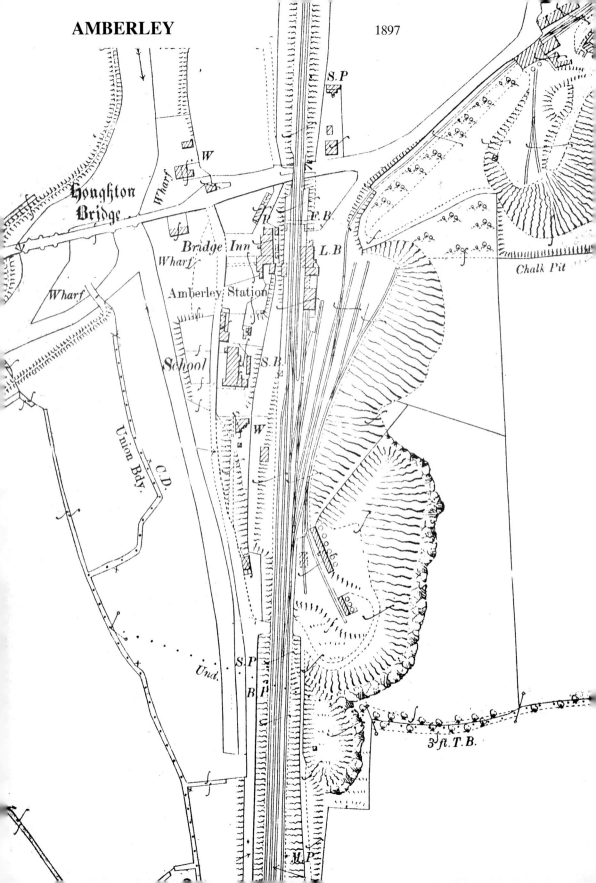

AMBERLEY

1897

Houghton Bridge

Wharf

W

S.P

I.B

Bridge Inn

Wharf

L.B

Amberley Station

Wharf

Wharf

R

School

S.B

W

Union Bdy.

C.D.

Chalk Pit

Und.

S.P

B.P

3 ft. T.B.

M.P

79. A postcard view looking north shows a station and goods shed of modest proportions, designed to match the needs of the district. The shed and the house were unfortunately lost in the BR clearance campaign. (Lens of Sutton)

80. Amberley church and castle are in the background as class D1 no. 268 runs towards the coast. The double arm signal post is stayed across the track to another post to prevent it slipping on the embankment. (F.W. Spry/E.R. Lacey collection)

81. Driver Hodge and Fireman Francis enjoy a break whilst shunting the yard in 1934. Signalling students can enjoy a rare view of the signal box in its original position, before operations were transferred to the booking office later that year. (F.G. Holmes)

83. Electric passenger services commenced on 30th June 1938 and here we witness the first public down train to this station. (F.G. Holmes)

82. South of the station two sidings entered the Balcombe Pit of Pepper & Son. There were nine limekilns in this pit and twenty in their larger pit north east of the station. The causeway and bridge over the Arun for the B2139 is on the left. Lineside power cables can be seen beside the light engine in the up siding but no conductor rails are visible which suggests a date of 1938 for this view. (J.W.R. Kirkby)

84. A footbridge was added in 1891 but earlier the line on the left had been laid into the main lime works from the goods yard. The pre-WWII cars do not help to date this picture which was taken on 17th July 1958. (D. Cullum)

85. Looking south on the same day we gain an impression of the track layout and a glimpse of the signal cabin under the awning. Hopefully funds can be found to conserve the charming up side building to prevent it being replaced by a characterless "bus shelter". (D. Cullum)

86. From April 1894 until August 1968, the
booking office doubled as a post office. Mr.
Jack Lisher is seen issuing the family allow-
ance and a day return to Littlehampton on
1st October 1962, although the Pulborough
station master was the registered post master!
Union opposition increased to the continued
operation of this efficient arrangement,
which was not a unique one in the south.
(British Rail)

87. For many years the SR provided camping coaches at the cattle dock, these examples in 1947 being ex-LCDR. Being located in a gap in the South Downs, the site is an excellent centre for walkers – many still come from the metropolis on Awayday tickets. (Lens of Sutton)

88. A photograph taken in November 1967 shows an improved standard of accommodation; a change of name and loss of the other sidings. Soon these coaches too were lost, being withdrawn nationwide as a matter of policy. (D. Cullum)

89. In 1986, the station had four semaphore signals in operation. The down starter was surprisingly on an ex-LSWR post. The crossover was retained for use by the engineers and was not controlled from the box. (V. Mitchell)

PEPPER & SON

90. Peppers inherited the chalk pits and lime kilns from a number of different operators in the immediate locality. Before the advent of the railway, their products had been distributed largely by canal boat – see *West Sussex Waterways* (Middleton Press). Peppers became general builders merchants with branches in many Sussex towns. The Balcombe Pit became a store yard and is seen here being shunted by their Aveling & Porter geared locomotive. Beside its flywheel, there is a pulley from which a belt drive could be taken to a crushing machine.
(CPM collection)

91. A view from about 1905 shows activity in the main pit with the other geared locomotive, an 1878 Marshall on the left. Details of the firms locomotives are given in *Industrial Railways of the South East* (Middleton Press) under photographs nos. 71 to 74. Lime was loaded direct into railway wagons at the kiln side, using special wheelbarrows, but production declined and ceased in the 1960s.
(CPM collection)

CHALK PITS MUSEUM

92. The 36-acre quarry was acquired by West Sussex County Council so that it could control closely the use of the site in this area of great natural beauty. In 1978 it was leased to the Southern Industrial History Centre Trust who are developing a most comprehensive exhibition of largely working relics. Of particular interest to the railway fraternity is the 2ft gauge railway collection, much of which was formerly stored at Brockham – hence the name of the station. The building for this was once a shelter for passengers on Brighton Corporation Tramways. The locomotive is 2–4–0T *Polar Bear*, built in 1905 by Bagnalls for the Groudle Glen line on the Isle of Man. (V. Mitchell)

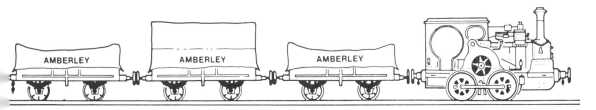

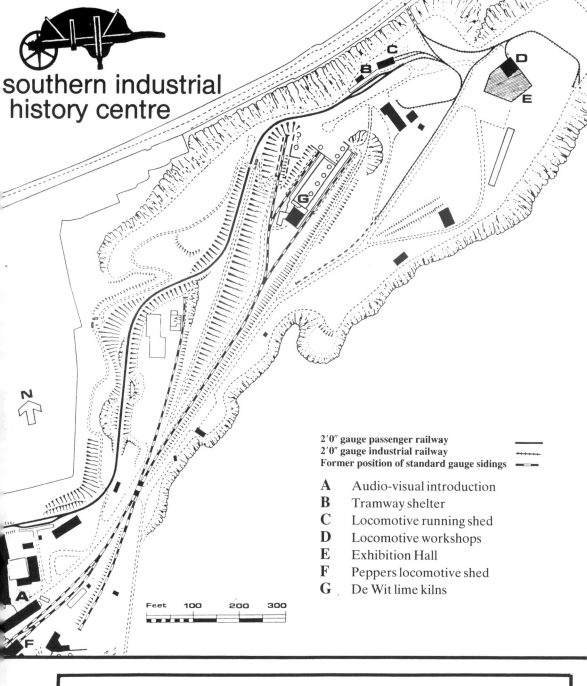

southern industrial history centre

2'0" gauge passenger railway ———
2'0" gauge industrial railway +++++
Former position of standard gauge sidings —·—

A   Audio-visual introduction
B   Tramway shelter
C   Locomotive running shed
D   Locomotive workshops
E   Exhibition Hall
F   Peppers locomotive shed
G   De Wit lime kilns

Feet   100   200   300

- narrow gauge industrial railway
- stationary oil and petrol engines
- blacksmith's shop
- printer's shop
- potter's workshop
- history of concrete exhibition
- motor bus garage and display
- vintage wireless exhibition
- tannery building
- brick industry exhibition
- boat-builder's workshop
- carpentry tools & machines
- water pumps
- metal-working machine shop
- vintage lawn mowers
- steam traction engines
  and road rollers
- museum and craft shop
- refreshment facilities

93. In 1986 a fine exhibition hall devoted to British narrow gauge industrial railway equipment was opened. Exhibits in view (from front to back) are Redland Orenstein & Koppel diesel; Dick Kerr side tipping skip; 27 Simplex; 26 London Brick Co. clay wagon; Penrhyn 2-ton slate wagon and a Festiniog Railway slate wagon.
(CPM collection)

94. The generous clearance in the 83yd North Stoke tunnel is evident as no. 33062 speeds south with a special train (Footex) from Liverpool to Hove on 29th January 1984. (J. Scrace)

95. Burpham box, seen here in 1965, was manned only when traffic density demanded, as at Thorndell. Two meanders in the River Arun nearby were cut off – one by the proprietors of the Arun Navigation and the other by the railway builders. (D. Cullum)

ARUNDEL

96. Since the days when horses left evidence of their earlier presence, the exterior has changed little. The entrance door has been moved to the right and a new plain canopy, sloping backwards, has been provided.
(Lens of Sutton)

1897

97. The opening of the goods yard was one factor causing the decline of Arundel as a port. With the increasing size of vessels Littlehampton developed at its expense, aided by the expansion of the railway wharves there. Points of interest are the variety of wagon owners and the timber

bolster by the 5-ton crane in the foreground, whilst on the skyline we see the Roman Catholic cathedral; the Anglican church (part of which was Catholic for the benefit of the Norfolk family) and the famous castle. (F.W. Spry/E.R. Lacey collection)

98. A condition in the sale of the land by the Duke of Norfolk for the construction of the railway was that all London trains should stop at Arundel. An opulent private waiting room was provided for the Duke. Class D1 no. 10 *Banstead* waits in the down bay with a Littlehampton and Bognor train, in 1902. (Lens of Sutton)

99. The "Littlehampton Shuttle" connected with many of the London expresses. It arrived at the up bay and, when empty, crossed to the down bay where the locomo- tive ran round the train, as we witness here. On the left, a cattle truck stands by the pens. (Lens of Sutton)

100. A 1914 photograph captures the arrival of a train from London Bridge behind a class I3 4–4–2T, whilst the branch train waits in the down bay. (Lens of Sutton)

101. Walter Vincent is portrayed in about 1930 in the LBSCR box seen in the earlier photographs. The SR replaced this box by one in "Odeon" style and BR has subsequently fitted it with a modern electronic signal panel which also controls part of the Coastway route from Lyminster to Ford, including Littlehampton Junction. (F.G. Holmes)

London Brighton & South Coast Railway.

Amberley to

Portsmouth Tn.

← 102. Looking south in 1930, the complicated trackwork is evident. Prior to electrification the platforms were more than doubled in length; the line next to the goods shed was lost and the up bay was fenced off, the track becoming part of the goods yard.
(Late E. Wallis)

→ 103. DMUs are a rarity on the line – these formed the 8.38 Slough to Bognor excursion on 8th June 1968. A band of mobile London Clay crosses the line near this 1938 signal box, hence the sheet steel piling seen on the left of the cutting. (E. Wilmshurst)

→ 104. The scene in 1974, showing a car park in the former goods yard, which had closed in September 1963. The down bay ceased to be used in 1972 and the track was lifted in 1977. In recent years, one train has started here each weekday – the 8.08 to Chichester.
(J. Scrace)

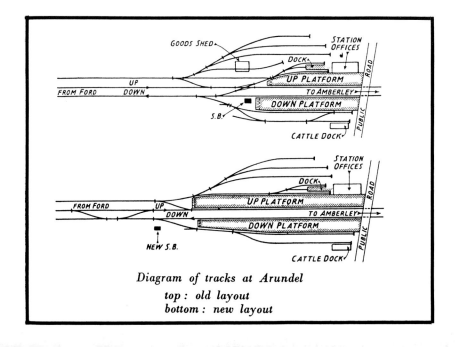

Diagram of tracks at Arundel

top : old layout
bottom : new layout

105. Having passed through one of the most beautiful areas in the South, the Mid-Sussex line (now more aptly, the Arun Valley line) joins the LBSCR West Coast route (now Coastway West) at Arundel Junction. This is seen from the top of the Down Brighton Home signal in 1929. After electrification, the signalman would have had little time to tend his nearby allotment. The diagram shows the frequency of the new service and the map indicates the 1887 alterations to the junctions. (Late E. Wallis)

106. The sub-station received a direct hit from enemy aircraft on 4th October 1940. During another raid, a German plane crashed in the soft ground behind the signal box. (British Rail)

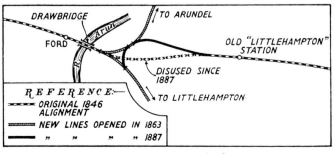

(Railway Magazine)

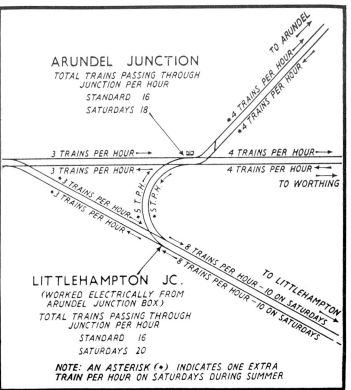

ARUNDEL JUNCTION

TOTAL TRAINS PASSING THROUGH
JUNCTION PER HOUR

STANDARD 16

SATURDAYS 18

TO ARUNDEL →

* 4 TRAINS PER HOUR

* 4 TRAINS PER HOUR

3 TRAINS PER HOUR → ⊠ | 4 TRAINS PER HOUR →

3 TRAINS PER HOUR ← | 4 TRAINS PER HOUR ←

TO WORTHING

* 3 TRAINS PER HOUR →

5 T.P.H. →

S.T.P.H. →

* 3 TRAINS PER HOUR ←

* 8 TRAINS PER HOUR

* 8 TRAINS PER HOUR – 10 ON SATURDAYS

TO LITTLEHAMPTON

LITTLEHAMPTON JC.

(WORKED ELECTRICALLY FROM
ARUNDEL JUNCTION BOX)

TOTAL TRAINS PASSING THROUGH
JUNCTION PER HOUR

STANDARD 16

SATURDAYS 20

NOTE: AN ASTERISK (*) INDICATES ONE EXTRA
TRAIN PER HOUR ON SATURDAYS DURING SUMMER

107. Basically similar to Arundel, the main building survived until 1937. Owing to disagreement with the local authority over the plans and the advent of WWII, its replacement was delayed. Work started in 1986, when the building on the left was finally demolished. (Author's collection)

108. The station bus was operated by Mr. Harris until about 1925. Back in 1887, a proposal was made for a mile long electric tramway to link the station with the sea front. (H.J.F. Thompson collection)

109. The engine shed dated from the opening of the line and was allocated up to ten locomotives in its prime. In 1937 it ceased its original function, serving as parcel office and staff accommodation, and will be retained in the 1986 redevelopment.
(E.R. Lacey collection)

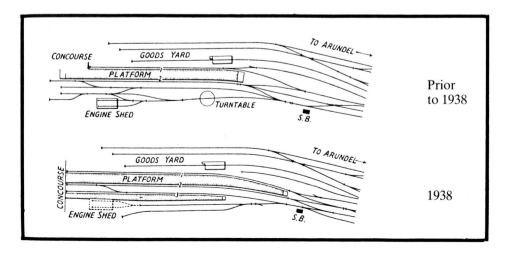

110. Class D3 0–4–4T no.268 was built in 1893 and ran over 1½ million miles before being withdrawn in 1952. Inexperienced travellers sometimes thought the name on the tank indicated the destination of the train. (E.R. Lacey collection)

112. At about the same time as the LBSCR introduced the rail motor service between Three Bridges and Horsham, a similar service commenced between Brighton and Worthing. This was extended to Little-hampton in 1907 and one such train is seen here in 1913, formed of 0–6–0T "Terrier" no. 680 with the characteristic high-roofed balloon coach. (Lens of Sutton)

Littlehampton traffic figures 1932

	Outwards	Inwards
Tickets ordinary	66,386	198,653
Tickets season	946	–
Tickets platform	937	–
Parcels	6,901	39,481
Milk (gallons)	6,580	22,719
General goods (tons)	2,091	5,168
Coal, coke (tons)	4,353	9,119
Minerals (tons)	23,228	2,158
Lavatory receipts £77*		

*This represents 18,480 visits

Tickets collected (1000s)

1927	238
1932	198
1938	287
1939	320
1942	225
1943	279
1957	539

111. Class B2 no. 212 *Armstrong* was rebuilt as a B2X in 1910 but on 21st July 1904 it suffered a derailment opposite the signal box. Three other B2s had been converted to oil firing in the previous year, using a steam injection system. (Lens of Sutton)

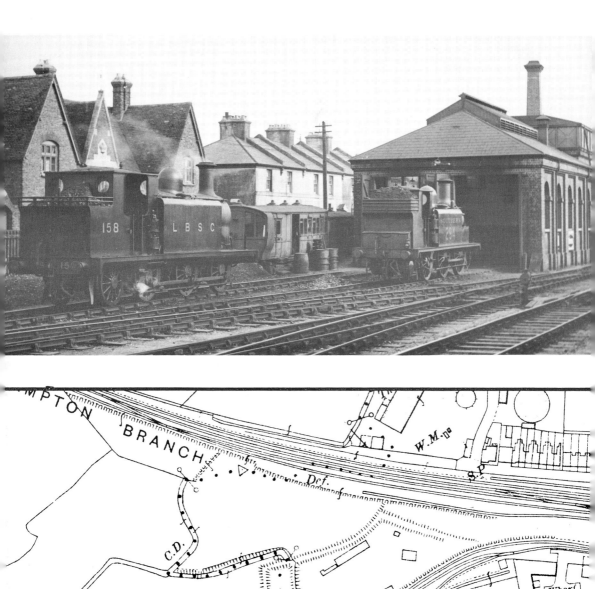

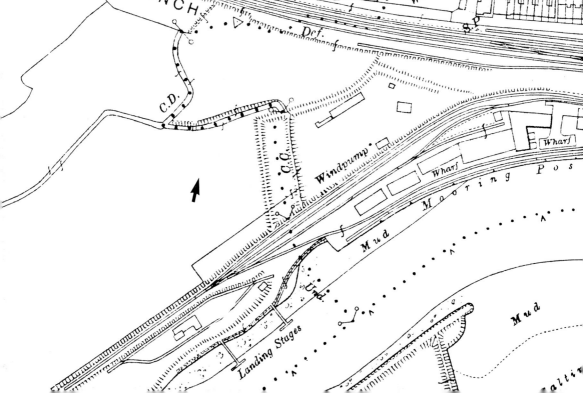

113. No.158 was in a class of its own when completed in 1891, being Stroudley's only radial tank engine. It was completed after his death, named *West Brighton* and is seen standing in front of the police station in February 1927. By then it had been modified to class E3. No.294 is a D-tank, built as *Rosebery* and renamed *Falmer* in 1897. (H.C. Casserley)

114. With only two platforms it was possible to photograph all the starting signals at once, prior to 1938. The ringed arms were shunt signals. The wharfside scene is in the background. (Lens of Sutton)

1932 edition

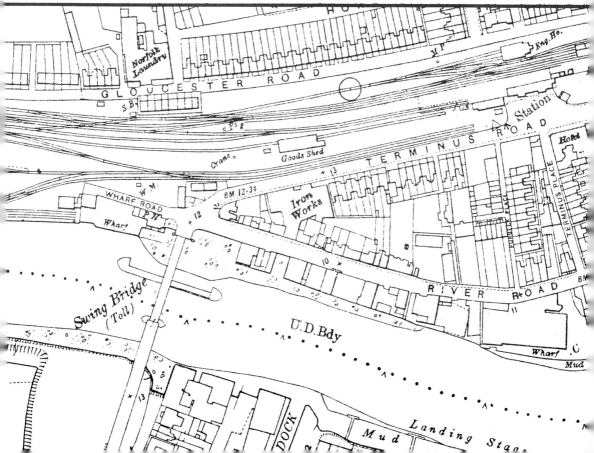

115. The station master appears stern, in his wing-collar and SR cap, whilst Mr. Bacon grins on the right. He was known locally as "Streaky". (H.J.F. Thompson collection)

117. Residents of Gloucester Road could enjoy watching the coaling and turning of locomotives, although this activity was much reduced with the end of regular steam passenger services. (E. Jackson)

OFFICIAL OPENING SOUTHERN RAILWAY ELECTRIFICATION
TO LITTLEHAMPTON. JUNE 30-1938
WHITE. PHOTO

116. Higher ranking officers arrive on 30th
June 1938 for the official opening of the
electrification scheme, many with the nearly
extinct wing collar. The first test train had
entered the station "on the juice" on 6th
February that year.
(H.J.F. Thompson collection).

118. In 1955 the wharf cranes consisted of a 6-ton Grafton (steam), a 2-ton Cowan (steam) and a 3-ton Stothert & Pitt (electric). The wharves are fully illustrated and described in our *Worthing to Chichester* album. (H.J.F. Thompson collection)

←

119. The Grafton was made at the Vulcan Works, Bedford, and is shown here in May 1967. The lines to the wharf were lifted to make way for a road to the new bridge, upstream from the swing bridge. The goods yard closed in May 1970. (D. Clayton)

→

121. An artist's impression gives an indication of the pleasant terminus that one will reach after the splendours of a journey over the Arun Valley line. (British Rail)

120. Locomotive hauled trains are now rare. This is 11.39 football special to Highbury on 16th April 1983, behind no. 33211. Three of the lines in the foreground enter the carriage shed and plans have been made to electrify the sidings on the right for stock storage. (E. Wilmshurst)

MP Middleton Press

Easebourne Lane, Midhurst, West Sussex, GU29 9AZ
☎ Midhurst (073 081) 3169

BRANCH LINES

BRANCH LINES TO MIDHURST	0 906520 01 0
BRANCH LINES TO HORSHAM	0 906520 02 9
BRANCH LINE TO SELSEY	0 906520 04 5
BRANCH LINES TO EAST GRINSTEAD	0 906520 07 X
BRANCH LINES TO ALTON	0 906520 11 8
BRANCH LINE TO HAYLING	0 906520 12 6
BRANCH LINE TO SOUTHWOLD	0 906520 15 0
BRANCH LINE TO TENTERDEN	0 906520 21 5
BRANCH LINES TO NEWPORT	0 906520 26 6
BRANCH LINES TO TUNBRIDGE WELLS	0 906520 32 0
BRANCH LINE TO SWANAGE	0 906520 33 9

SOUTH COAST RAILWAYS

BRIGHTON TO WORTHING	0 906520 03 7
WORTHING TO CHICHESTER	0 906520 06 1
CHICHESTER TO PORTSMOUTH	0 906520 14 2
BRIGHTON TO EASTBOURNE	0 906520 16 9
RYDE TO VENTNOR	0 906520 19 3
EASTBOURNE TO HASTINGS	0 906520 27 4
PORTSMOUTH TO SOUTHAMPTON	0 906520 31 2

SOUTHERN MAIN LINES

WOKING TO PORTSMOUTH	0 906520 25 8
HAYWARDS HEATH TO SEAFORD	0 906520 28 2
EPSOM TO HORSHAM	0 906520 30 4
CRAWLEY TO LITTLEHAMPTON	0 906520 34 7

STEAMING THROUGH

STEAMING THROUGH KENT	0 906520 13 4
STEAMING THROUGH EAST HANTS	0 906520 18 5
STEAMING THROUGH EAST SUSSEX	0 906520 22 3

OTHER RAILWAY BOOKS

WAR ON THE LINE The official history of the SR in World War II	0 906520 10 X
GARRAWAY FATHER AND SON The story of two careers in steam	0 906520 20 7

OTHER BOOKS

MIDHURST TOWN – THEN & NOW	0 906520 05 3
EAST GRINSTEAD – THEN & NOW	0 906520 17 7
THE GREEN ROOF OF SUSSEX A refreshing amble along the South Downs Way	0 906520 08 8
THE MILITARY DEFENCE OF WEST SUSSEX	0 906520 23 1
WEST SUSSEX WATERWAYS	0 906520 24 X
BATTLE OVER PORTSMOUTH A City at war in 1940	0 906520 29 0